Second Chances

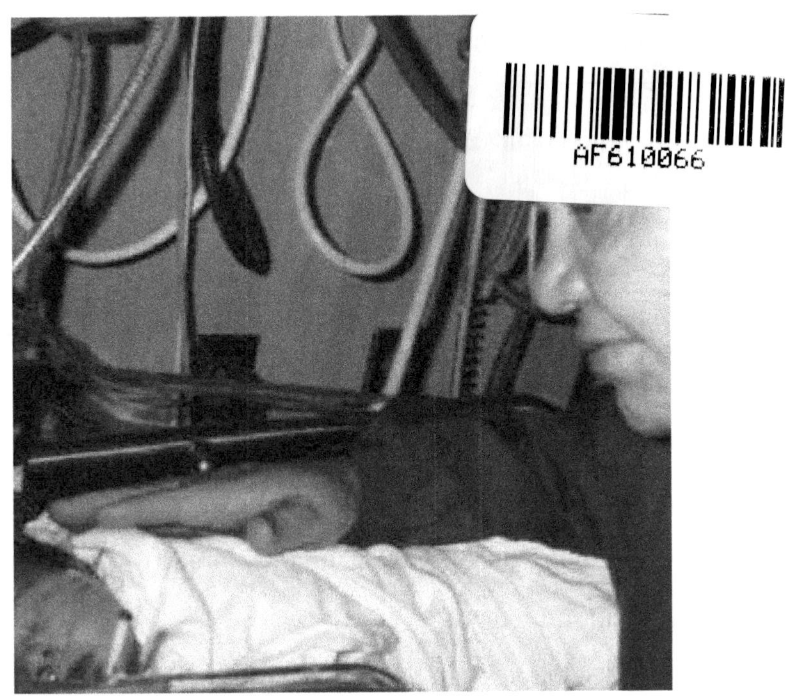

Miracles can happen

By Alexis Gutierrez

Second Chances

All scripture quotations, are taken from the King James Bible online ® copyright © 2019.

The italics in the scripture quotation reflect the author's choice.

Cover design by Alexis Gutierrez

Names: Gutierrez, Alexis, 1997- author.

Title: Second Chances / Alexis Gutierrez.

Description: First Edition. Sterling ,Colorado : / Includes bibliographical references.

Subjects: Miracles can happen. - Religious Aspects- Christianity.

Printed in the United States of America

2019 _ First Edition

Dedication

This book is dedicated to my parents and family for always believing in me. And pushing me to work hard to accomplish my goals.

And to my beloved Third- Grade teacher Mrs. Robin Grant. Who taught me to pursue my dreams. Trust in God because he can fix the impossible.

The Flashback

I remember the first time I met her I was so shy and afraid. But right then I knew I could trust her and all my fears went away. Right as I walked into that bright yellow Bumble Bee room. I saw Mrs. Grant my new Third-Grade teacher. She had such a smile that just lightened up the room when you walked in. But then we were inseparable and the best of friends. Even though she was my teacher she was my best friend and my mentor. I could tell her anything and she would just know what to say. She shared the best advice and wisdom.

Even though I had her for an extra year that was the best two years of my life. And after I went on to the other grades she was the only teacher who cared and kept in touch with me through the years and I am very thankful for all of our memories and lunch in the classroom. And she was the only one to inspire me to keep writing my short stories. Even though they were not in complete sentences or the best handwriting. She always told me to ignore what others think.

To her I was a miracle from God. And that my writing was a gift. I just wish she was here to help me but I know without her encouragement this book would not be possible.

I would have never wanted to be a teacher if it was not for her kindness and compassion that she had towards me and her faith. She inspired so many of her students and how we always wrote to each other. When she would sub I would visit and we would catch up with each other. But I would not have started writing if she did not encourage my passion.

That is why my beloved and cherished teacher this book was dedicated to you I wish you could be here to see it but I know you are smiling from above.

Introduction

This is a true story about a little girl who was born in a world where her parents were told she wouldn't make it. This is the hardest thing to tell any parent, especially teen parents. Her parents refused to let her take her last breath. So they had all their friends and family and church to pray for the baby. They believed that she would survive.

Breana had to have surgery to fix the two holes in heart. She had open heart surgery and corration repair . They flew her to another hospital where her crazy journey began. Literally, her life was hanging in the balance. But she survived that surgery when the doctors said she would die. Where they had to open her front chest to fix the holes. The doctors left her chest open for a few days. And then on her left upper shoulder they had to go in . So she has two scars from her surgery. She was hooked up to an incubator with a bunch of chords helping her breathe. She was like that for two months.

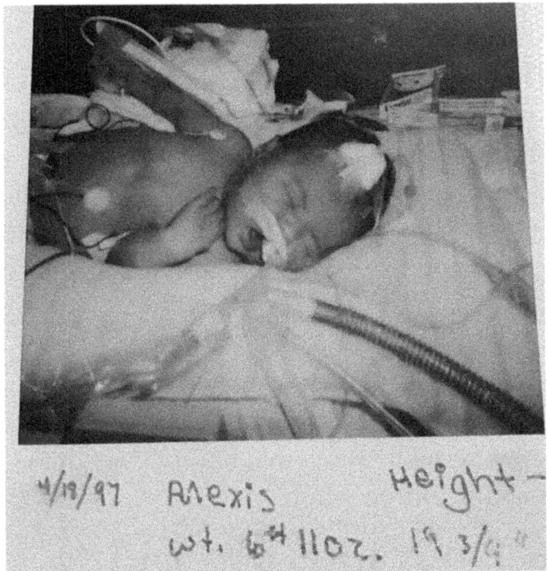

Now she is a twenty two year old woman.

God had another plan in store right from the beginning. He knew she would be here today way before she came into the world. Before she was a tiny seed just waiting to be formed into a tiny person.

Like in the book of Jeremiah verse
29 :11 Says "For I know the plans I have for you, declares the Lord. Plans to prosper you and not to harm you, plans to give you hope and future."

She is glad and thanks God that she was given a second chance. She knows she has some struggles that she had to overcome. That you will learn about with having complications from the start to even her adult life. But those struggles have not stopped her from doing anything.

As long as she puts her mind to something she can accomplish anything. Her life was not very easy but she persevered through all the tough obstacles in her way. And when everyone doubted her and said she can't do something she did it anyway.

Just like in the bible. With the story of Esther or (Hadassah) she freed all her people. Even when she thought she could not succeed. She did. She had enough courage to finally stand before the king. Even though she knew she could be killed because it was against the law to speak before the king. But in the end she saved all her people. Even when she was afraid and Haman was trying to stop her. God had a plan in store for her and her people right from the beginning when she was chosen to be the queen.

The story of David and Goliath where everyone laughed at him .Since he was so small. As long as he believed he could and that God had his back he could defeat the giant. And he flung that big rock and hit Goliath and the head defeating him and all his people.

1

The Unexpected News

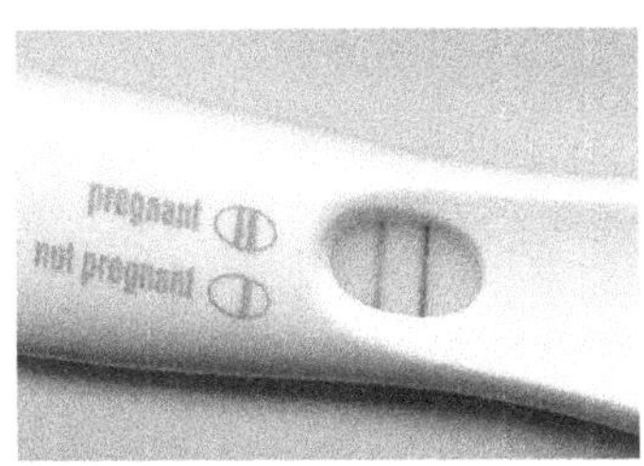

There was a young teen couple who were madly in love and who didn't expect to become teen parents. They were still in High School. And only fifteen and seventeen. She was the most beautiful baby girl. She was born on April 14, 1997. In Sterling Colorado at the hospital . She weighed six pounds , thirteen ounces. God had given them her name is Breana.

They would soon find out that something was wrong with their baby girl. She was having trouble breathing so the nurse told them she was not going to make it and to tell her goodbye.

Her parents believed in God and that she would be fine. Also, her Great Grandmother Ofelia prayed and laid her hand over her that she would make it despite what the doctors told her parents. Also, her parent's pastors and the whole church prayed that she would pull through the surgery.

So, they had to fly her to another hospital to correct her two holes in her heart. The doctors did not think she would make it. But she fought and proved them wrong and survived. She was on oxygen and in the incubator in the hospital recovering for two months before her family could take her home. But even though she survived the surgery the doctors did tell her parents that in the future she could have complications.

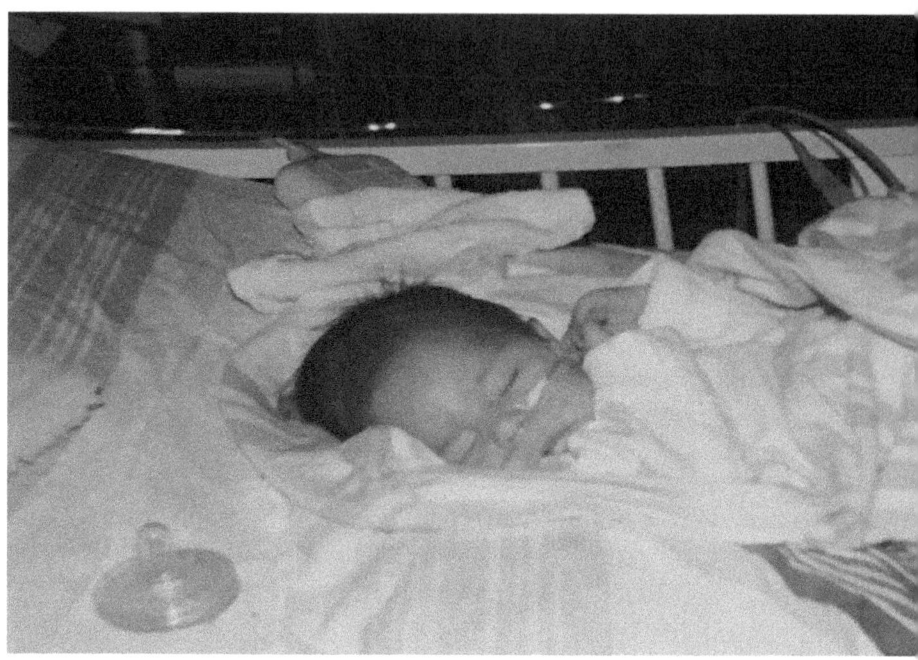

Her family didn't care she was perfect in their eyes. And that she was special and just thankful that God had saved her. So that one day she could do anything she puts her mind to.

2
The Learning Struggle

In preschool she struggled and they wanted her parents to hold her back but they didn't. By the time she was in the Third - Grade she was struggling and getting bad grades. That the principal and Third - Grade teacher decided she should be held back. It was not fun to have to relearn everything.

It was all worth it to get to spend time with her amazing teacher Mrs. Grant. Who taught her a lot of things that she will never forget. She was the first teacher who was a friend and was kind and helped her succeed. Who believed in her and inspired her to write.

So, to this day she is very thankful to have had such an amazing strong woman of God. She is smiling down from heaven. Breana wishes that she could be here so they can talk to each other. And give her advice when she needs it. She knows that she is making her proud by accomplishing her dreams.

After she was held back she went on to the next grade but she was still struggling with math. Where it would be so frustrating for her and parents. Where they could not figure out why their precious daughter could not understand.

Then she finally got into her last two years of High School she was tested. And finally found out why all the math concepts she could not grasp was because she had a learning disability. Also has an IEP, she received extra help with homework and tests and quizzes. By the time it was her senior year, she had to work extra hard to understand the concepts. So, she went to after school math help with Mrs. Pinder. She studied extra hard and passed math with passing grades. And accomplished her most challenging subject and proved that she can do anything. Still to this day she has a hard time understanding simple math equations.

And it could be very frustrating at times. The kids would ask a math question and she could not help them because she did not understand.

That is not the only class she struggled in. She also had a hard time with English. But she always got average grades with that subject. Except for her last year she was struggling trying to manage getting a C. In the class and it also didn't help that her teacher picked on her. He made a whole lesson about her in front of the whole class. It was the most embarrassing thing any teacher ever did to her. Then she cried like a baby. He made her angry and upset. And made it hard for her to try to pass. Because she was shy and didn't like to participate that much or ask questions. Breana proved him wrong and passed not with the best grade on the final exam. It was hard having her learning disabilities. She had trouble with reading certain books or articles. But that does not mean she gave up.

She recently finished a book that was 200 pages. Most people they would have finished it very quickly. But she had to take her time to understand the concepts and read some of the pages over again.

So, it is okay to struggle with some subjects because nobody is perfect. Every person struggles with something different but don't let that struggle bring you down. Take it and conquer it and don't let it define who you are. And keep pushing forward toward your goals. Then you will succeed and stand tall.

3
The Final mile

Although, your last year of High School is supposed to be the best she had some ups and downs. But she also joined a club where she was writing for the school paper and coming out of her shy little shell. She is glad she joined and got to share her talent with others and meet new people. And she went to Kent State for a day for a journalism club awards night. She didn't win any awards but it was still a great experience to be a part of.

Lastly, she did the one thing no one thought she would ever do. She tried out for a school sport on her last year of school. Which a lot of people think that is crazy unless she was athletic or something.

But honestly, she had not had any physical activity for four years. So, it was very challenging to get back in shape. She showed up on the first day of practice and it was kind of weird. Because all the other Seniors on the team were not very welcoming but the younger students were helpful.

A lot of students would tell her middle sister that she was awful and she should quit. But that just motivated her to want to work more at home and in practice.

She was able to run with her best friend Morgan so it was really cool . And she encouraged her and pushed her to do better and showed her what to do . Because she has been on track for a while so she knew what to do. And what each term meant when they were at practice or at a meet. And how to use the track starters so you are not disqualified. And they got to run in the same line up sometimes . And how not to get a false start when the gun sounded off. That means they ran in the same starting row. But her friend always ran faster. It didn't matter since they were on the same team and best friends.

By the time it was meets she was improving and her coach's noticed. Soon they started letting her run 4 events. Which to her was a big deal because that is a lot of running and very stressful on her body, but she didn’t hesitate she may have never got in 1 ,2 ,3 place but she still keep pushing to do the best she could. She injured her right leg. The doctors checked it and said she was fine. But she was still in pain.

On her last final meet which was away she beat her P.R. in the 200 and the 100. And almost beat one of her teammates who were faster than her. She gave it her all with blood sweat, tears and pain. She accomplished another thing that a lot of people doubted her but she persevered through it.

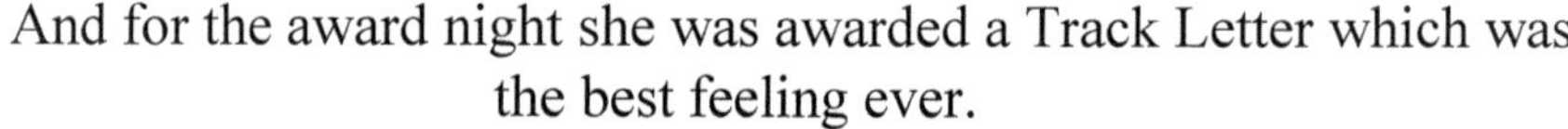

And for the award night she was awarded a Track Letter which was the best feeling ever.

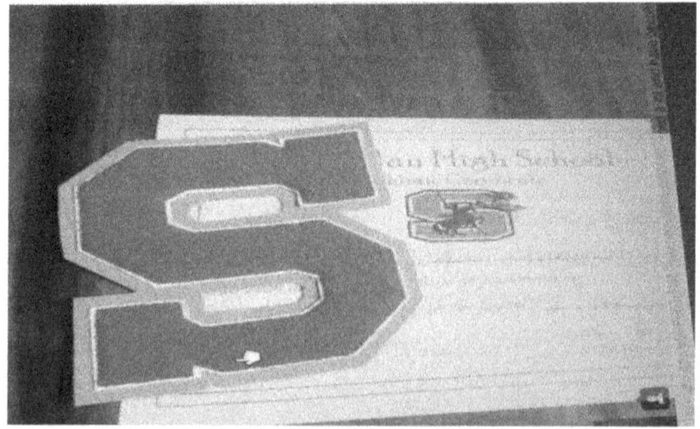

To know that all her hard work and dedication finally paid off. But her leg still affects her very much so she finally went to see a physical therapist to fix the problem. So, she can go back to doing normal exercises and hopefully being able to run a marathon or race one day. But for now, she is finally accomplished the big milestone and conquered High School.

4
Real Life Begins

She was working at a daycare down the street from her house. Because she still does not have her driver's license. She walked to work which was really hard because her pain in her leg was affected. She worked about like 24 /7. She had her own house. And if she wants to buy other things she can with her extra money.

She worked with Pre-K students. So, she made lesson plans and games and gave them candy. But she also worked with the babies, Toddlers, and School - Agers. She could have 12 students all by herself, which is a lot to handle but she made it work.

She went to church on Sundays with her family. The best church she has ever gone to in her entire life. It is just amazing they have great worship team so she enjoys all the songs. Especially when they bring out their rappers who can spit words for God is pretty cool. The worship team has two albums. So her favorite song to listen to is *Hope Has Come* by One Church Music.

And she likes how she can relate to the messages from the Bible to her own life. And that it is not just a long boring church day it is fun and exciting and upbeat. And if she misses a service she can always listen to the podcast later. And she loves how relevant the church is with social media and she looks forward to going every Sunday. And she can actually understand the message and wants to listen to it over and over, unlike most services where she rather blocks it out or think about something else.

She reads her Bible and prays when she needs God's help. But the one thing that helps her every day is Philippians 4:13 "I can do all things through Christ who gives me strength." (KJV). This verse really has such a strong meaning for her especially when she was in school and wanted to give up to keep pushing and she would make it.

When she ran track even in pain and people saying she was not good enough. She proved them wrong with her faith and trust in God. It also helps her when she is having a tough time to remember she can achieve anything that seems complicated. She has conquered a lot of things that others thought were impossible. She may be a little shy but that does not stop her from doing what she wants.

5
Family is Life

Her family is everything to her. They are there when she needs them for her support system. She has two younger sisters who are 17and 7. They are the best siblings ever they can get on her nerves but that happens with every family. She loves each of them so much.

They each have different personalities and she can see some of herself in them. She loves to spoil them but that is what big siblings are for. She loves spending time with them.

With her younger sister they like to watch wrestling together. She got her a diva belt and then they like to reenact the matches. They love to watch everything that is WWE with each other and their dad. But at the daycare
on certain days she used to see her little sister. And she was her teacher in the afternoon.

Allyah loves to shop especially online. She likes to shop till you drop on all the deals to her favorite store which is Pink. Her sister is all about the fashions and current trends in the world.

Breana is the total opposite she likes more guy things. Like wrestling and football and soccer. And UFC fighting on Saturdays .

But she also misses her baby brother Ezekiel who would have been 19 this year. He passed away shortly after he was born because his lungs collapsed. So, to honor his memory on her 18th birthday she got her first tattoo.

It is six inches on her upper shoulder. It is angel wings that are around the baby shoes like a heart and his name on top.

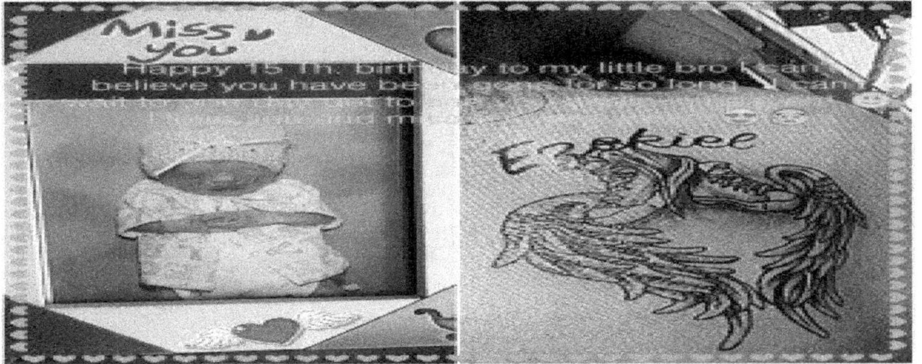

She keeps his baby picture from the hospital on her black night stand. She looks at it every day and night and can't wait until they can see each other again.

She got her second tattoo recently it is the scripture Philippians 4:13 inside the teal blue infinity sign. It is on her left forearm.

But her family is very special and dear to her they have helped her and molded her to be the person she is today. She is a strong and independent woman. She has a loving and caring personality.

On Sundays is family day where they all go to church and go shopping or out to eat. Or they watch a movie on their indoor movie theater.

This is their most recent photo from this year .

6
Hobbies and Collections

She has a few hobbies which are way different than other girls or women. Breana loves football which was said earlier. So as one of her favorite things is to watch football and cheer on her favorite NFL team the Denver Broncos and to cheer on Ohio State Buckeyes.

But one hobby is collecting football cards which most people would think that is kind of odd for a girl. So far, she has collected about four card binders and her total amount of cards is 2,488.

She also has some baseball and basketball cards too. But there is way more football cards . She started collecting cards when a sports store at the mall had dollar grab bags. The cards were in a brown sandwich bag .
They would have random football players from different NFL teams.
And some college teams and rookie cards. Her one card is of Anthony Gonzalez. Who used to dated one of her cousins. She met him and went to his apartment. He was really nice and a big guy. But he had to retire from the NFL because of an injury.

Also, she has two football posters and Peyton Manning jersey and his Lego and a Bronco license plate. Also, a Bronco beer can and a key chain. And she recently got a Denver Bronco cereal box from her grandparents. She plans to collect a lot more things but that is not the only things she loves to collect.

She also is a huge wrestling fan so she collects fan merchandise especially for her favorite women wrestler Nikki Bella one of the Bella Twins. She has her hat and two shirts and the Bella Twins Pop characters. And she has a blue John Cena sweat towel with matching wristbands. They have his logo on them that says Never Give UP. Her wrestling collection is growing and she is running out of room to store it .

She also has a few comic books . They are mostly WWE but she has one Wonder Woman comic. Because she is the best female superhero ever created. And a Harley Quinn one because she is her favorite DC Comic villian. Also she collects DC Comics action figures . She has Harley Quinn and the Joker . Because she loves the movie *Suicide Squad.* And she has the Wonder Woman Pop Action figure from the movie.

She also has a few other wrestling items from this awesome website called Loot Crate. She gets a bunch of collectibles and memorabilia every six months.That she can cancel your subscription at any time. She has had seven boxes of wrestling merchandise so far. In each box she receives a shirt from a different wrestler. Different action figures every crate. And tiny wrestling belt pins that she can wear on a shirt. And in all of her wrestling collectibles she has a total of twenty action figures.

And her final thing she loves to collect is the Collector Pennies. Which she has a bunch of them from different Zoos and from SeaWorld and some water parks. Like Kalahari and Great Wolf Lodge in Cincinnati. Which are in cool machines they cost fifty one cents. She has four penny books that she stores the pennies in. Each of the books comes from a different place. She has one from Sea World. It has two huge black killer whales on it. Because that is what the theme park is known for. It is the Second Edition of the coin album. And she has one that is from the Columbus Zoo. It is a first edition. It has four different animals on the cover. The animals are an elephant, Otter, Manatee, and Tiger.

And her very first one to start her collection has the Bald Eagle on it. With the United States flag in the background and it's a Second Edition. Also, each coin album has one coin attached to it. The Eagle one has an American flag coin on the cover.

And the Zoo has a Bowhead shark on it. And the Sea World one has the killer whale coin on the cover. Each coin album can hold a total of thirty six collector pennies.
She recently went to Estes Park with her family and at one of the shops got two large Gold collector coins and more penny press coins from Estes park too.

But her main hobby is writing where she can let loose and be creative. She can write down her feelings and tell a story. She also likes to write to inspire people to follow their dreams. And to not let people tell you that you can't do what you want to. She has been writing for 10 years her passion developed in third grade. She had to write stories about princesses and princes and make-believe characters. Where she could let her imagination flow on a piece of paper and come to life. She would write them down in composition notebooks that are in her bedroom. And she wishes her handwriting was a lot better so she can read some of them. She would not have continued her passion for writing without the help of her third grade teacher Mrs. Grant. Who taught her everything she knows about writing and following your dreams until you achieve success. She will be truly grateful to have her two years in a row.

She wants to help her legacy live on through her. And hopefully with all of her other students that she inspired and made a difference in their lives.

Also, she loves to watch TV. She watches a lot of Medical Dramas like Grey's Anatomy, and Chicago Med, Pd. Fire. Those shows are fascinating with the drama and action and love lives. But she watches so many shows it is hard to pick her number one show.

Also since she loves wrestling so much she watches Total Divas and Total Bellas.

Also, she loves to listen to music, especially when she is writing it helps her relax and think and let her thoughts flow onto the page. She listens to Rap and R&B and Pop and Soulful music.

She likes Lecere for how real his music is and how she can relate to it in her life. For Lecrae she listens to "I will find you" feat. Tori Kelly. Because of his part and just the sound of the song is catchy.

From each artist she has her top song that she listens to over and over again until it gets stuck in her head.

And for Mariah Carey song "Bye Bye." She has listened to this particular song since she was eight years old. Because when she lost her great grandma she needed something to help her cope with her loss. So, this song helps to remind her of all the good times and memories that they got to share together. And her grandma will always be with her forever and she will cherish every day they had together.

But she also listens to Mexican American late singer Selena Quintanilla. The reason why she listens to her and knows about her music is because her dad was a huge fan . When Breana was born she was almost named after the late singer. She has two original collectible dolls of the late singer from her dad. They have never been opened .

And one doll is wearing her iconic purple outfit that she wore at her last concert in Houston Astrodome on February 26, 1995. The outfit has silver sparkles all over it . And the doll is holding a tiny microphone , And it comes with a purple hair brush and silver high heels. Her second doll is wearing the outfit wear Selena won her first Grammy one of the most prestigious awards in the recording industry. The dress is white with silver sparkles . And the doll comes with a silver purse and a white hairbrush. Each of the hairbrushes has her name on it.

She also has a Muluan collectible doll from the Disney movie . It is made by Mattel . And the doll is wearing a dress that is pink and blue . And has leaf designs and teal swirls on the top .

When she has free time, she likes to color which may be silly since she is all grown up now. But it is in adult coloring books. This helps to relieve stress and helps free her mind. She colors and it kind of brings back a feeling of her childhood of the good easy times. Where you could color outside the lines and everything was okay.

She loves to play video games when she has extra free time. They are fun she likes the graphics on the games when she plays against her family she gets very competitive. She gets this from her dad. Her all time favorite is Mario Brothers. Because it is cool and four people can play at a time. And you have to save princess Peach from Bowser. And you get to collect coins and if you get all of them in each level you can unlock the special world. That has extra levels in it.

She likes a lot of other games too that she plays on her different game systems. She has a Wii u and Wii, Sega, Nintendo Ds, Nintendo game system, Xbox. On her Xbox she has a WWE game where she can pretend to be the wrestlers and fight in the ring.

And recently for her 22 b day she got the Nintendo Switch from her parents. Which she has the Donkey Kong and Mario Kart games .

7
The Book

Breana is not very fond of reading but recently she just bought Tim Tebow's new book "*Shaken.*" So far one of the best reads she has read and can't keep it down. It is about Tim's football career and about finding your identity. And to not let other people define you.

But this book is also going along with her church message as well about finding your identity. So, for her this is helping her figure out the bumps on the road to lead her on the right path that God wants her to follow. Because right now she has found herself stuck and not knowing what direction she should turn next. She has so many gifts and passions but she doesn't know how to use them. She wants a sign to come out of nowhere to tell her what the next step is.

A lot of people tell her what they think she should do next and she has listened to their advice and opinions but does not feel that is what God is calling her to do. She does not want to just work and work until she is burned out and unhappy.

Because she has these special gifts and desires that drive her to use them but then she freezes. She feels like she is walking on a thin piece of ice about to break. It is her deep insecurity to try to please everyone instead of doing what she wants. She is afraid of what they will think instead of just seizing her moment. And take the chance of failing or becoming successful. But instead she just hides behind the crowd like a lost cloud.

A lot of people have doubted her in the past. Her fear is if she tries to go toward her dream and goal she will be put down. Over and over again, like she is losing a fight. Then she will be broken and shattered like a window hit by a baseball. Then she will have kept her pain inside until she has to find the strength to keep going. When she feels down, and tries to pick herself back up again. And to find her confidence to be the person she wants to be.

And to ignore what others want and do what her heart leads her to do. Even if she succeeds or fails at least she tried because you only live once. So, take the chance until you have your last dance.

She has come so far from being a shy quiet little kid who could barely speak to people. Finally she is emerging out of her shell. Just like when you see a hermit crab coming out of the shell. On the nice warm and blazing hot sandy beach.

By being a teacher, it was kind of a challenge. But she was trying to be the best teacher she could be. She wanted to make an impact on her students' lives. She knows that her late teacher Mrs. Grant would be very proud of her for being a teacher. And is smiling down from heaven. She made such a huge impact in her life.

By becoming a teacher Breana carried her legacy on. Also to be faithful to God to inspire many people just as her teacher did. Breana would have never thought she could be a teacher, so many people have doubted her ability but she just kept pushing forward. To use her true calling and passion that she has from God.

8
The Reflection in the Mirror

Now she looks in the mirror to reflect on everything she has overcome. From the beginning of life, it has always been a struggle. But no matter what she faced she persevered and kept going. Even though a lot of people have doubted her she proved them wrong. She pushed through all the pain.

And sometimes in the mirror she saw shattered pieces of glass. While others laughed at her in class. They didn't get why she was so shy. But she wished they would help her fix those broken pieces of glass. But no one could see her inside of the mirror. She felt trapped by her own reflection.

Just like with the Disney movie *Mulan.* She is not the person that she sees in her reflection. Because she is trying to please her family by being someone she is not. She does not want to dishonor her family name.

So be the reflection you want to be not what other people think you should be.

The Pop Legend Michael Jackson's song is the Man in the Mirror. It says if you want to make a change with yourself to do it. Only you have the power to change yourself.

Now she can see clearly in the mirror of who she is supposed to be. Because when no one cared God picked up the broken pieces. She would have to struggle to tell her story to help others. When others feel like they are broken and wanting to give up.

She knows that you have to trust God and eventually everything that you have to go through happens for a reason. Like Breana was given a second chance for a very special reason. So, God could use her one day.

Because when doctors said she would not make it God saved her. Because he knew she was born for a purpose. So go find your purpose and pursue it.
In Romans 8:28 "And we know that all things work together for good to them that love God, to them who are according to their purpose."

9
New Beginnings

Sometimes when you start something new it can be scary and frightening. When it's' time to change directions we as people panic. But that is okay. We get so used to doing the same thing like we are trapped in a door. But when we decide to open the door to a new path the panic flowing through your veins slowly goes away. And you start to breathe normal again.

As Breana's new path is totally different and is pushing her way out of her comfort zone. She knows she will be alright as long as she does the best. And prays that God has everything in control. As she taught her students they had some awesome moments that she will cherish in her heart forever. She will miss all of their laughs and hugs and cute smiles.

And all of the cool crafts and games they were able to do together. She is thankful to have been able to teach them and make such a positive impact in their lives.

She knows Mrs. Grant would be so proud of the teacher she became. To know her promise to her will be fulfilled one day. At the right time and place. And when it is all finished she will know she never gave up even when others said it would be impossible. But nothing is impossible even when others say you can't do something. Always follow your heart and do it anyway. She knows the promise is taking way longer than she wanted it too. She just has not been able to find a person or company to help turn her dream and promise into a reality yet. Hopefully one day the promise will be on the store shelves and she can be a successful writer just like she has always dreamed. Ever since she began writing at nine years old. When other people did not think she had a gift for writing.

Mrs. Grant was the only one to ever push her to keep going. Breana wishes she was still here to give her advice on what to do. And that this door is closing for a reason. As she start a new season.

10
The Holidays

It's the most wonderful time of the year as you start to hear Christmas jingles in the stores. And all the Christmas trees and lights and decors start to come on the shelves. Breana favorite holiday is Christmas.

She gets to spend the day with her family in matching Pjs. And take a family photo to put on social media. Also, getting to eat all the delicious food her dad prepares. And making the yummy sugar cookies with her siblings and making a mess in the kitchen. All the cookies are different shapes like Christmas items and trees and snowmen. And you get to decorate them with different color of frosting and to top it off with the best part sprinkles.

She loves eating her dad's amazing and delicious and giant popcorn balls. He makes delicious caramel popcorn. Getting to watch all the Christmas movies with her family. Like *Elf* and *Christmas with the Kranks, Home Alone Movies. The Santa Clause Movies* with actor Tim Allen. Her all time favorite Christmas comedy Four *Christmases.*

And she enjoys watching the white and fluffy snow fall down from the sky. As she sees it through the glass window . It is like living in a winter wonderland. Also she makes a delicious nice cup of warm hot cocoa, with marshmallows on top. She wraps herself in a big cozy blanket.

As you sit around the Christmas tree opening presents. It is so exciting to see all the fun gifts you received. But she likes to see her siblings faces light up when they get the gift they wanted.

But the main reason is celebrating the birth of Jesus. It is the day he was born with a purpose and had to make the biggest sacrifice for our sins.

11
The New Year

The New Year is approaching very fast. It is almost time to watch the ball drop at midnight on New Year's Eve. When many people start to plan their new dreams and goals, but they don't always achieve them. Breana knows what she wants her new goals to be. She hopes that she will be able to achieve them.

And not to fail or to make silly ones where people try to diet and then they give up. But she wants to make her goals simple and realistic. So that she can achieve and conquer them.

So her first goal is to finally go get her driver's license. To be able to move out again. She is currently living at home with her parents.

And to finally make her promise to Mrs. Grant come true. She is so close she can almost reach and grasp it. Just like you reach for the stars as many people say. She is a fingertip away in making her dream and promise finally a reality. Instead of just a simple thought she had a few years ago.

12
The Celebrations

Well this is going to be huge her youngest sister is turning six . She can't believe it she is growing up way too fast. She remembers changing her diapers and feeding her when she was just a baby. And now is going to turn six. For her birthday Ady wants a *Moana* cake and cupcakes.

Breana already bought the presents from her list. Some Cabbage Patch Lil Sprouts. Breana hopes her little sister will enjoy all of her gifts. And that her sister will have an amazing 6th birthday. This year she is going to be eight .

But that's not the only big birthday coming up. Her other sister Allyah is finally going to be 16. She wants to have a sweet sixteen. And have all her friends come over for a huge sleepover. Which is crazy Breana remembers when she was only 16. Time goes by so fast. She is now 17 .

And finally the biggest celebration of all is Breana is finally going to be the big 21. But hopefully it will be amazing as everyone says it is. To finally be classified as the real adult. She wants to go to Dave and Busters for her birthday. Because it has the biggest arcade with tons of games. And you can win tons of tickets to get awesome prizes from the ticket shop. In order to play the games you have to get a game card. That has points that you use to play the games you swipe the card to play. She wants to play deal or no deal. And the game that has fish on the side. It is where you pull a black lever and it spins numbers and wherever it lands thats how many tickets you get. Recently when she went to the Great Wolf Lodge with her family and she played in the arcade. And she won 1000 tickets for the first time ever. By playing that fish game with the black lever. She has played that game many times before but never has won so many tickets. So when the pointer landed on the 1000 tickets she though she only won four. Because it has four tickets and also 1000. So then all the tickets came out and she felt really lucky and like a kid again. Like when you get candy from a candy shop as a kid.

Or like in *Charlie and the Chocolate Factory* the movie. When Charlie uses his money from his grandparents. And he buys the candy bar that has the golden ticket in it. And he is one of the lucky kids to visit the chocolate factory to see Willy Wonka.

13
The Favorite Animal

Breana's favorite animal is a monkey. Because they are cute and very smart. They can swing from trees . Just like you can swing on monkey bars. And they have a lot of similar traits as humans do.

Plus there are many different kinds of monkey species. And they love to eat bananas which is one of Bre's favorite fruits. Also there are large monkeys and small ones. And they are all different colors and each have a different name. There are 260 living monkey species . Like the Gorilla which is enormous and then the tiniest is the Pygmy Marmoset. Her favorite money is the Chimpanzee. She loves watching the movie *Planet of the Apes* because it is all about monkeys. And how they can talk to each other. To fight a war against humankind. She loves going to the Zoo to see the monkey exhibit. Where all the monkeys are located . Each exhibit has a different kind. And she likes how the monkeys carry their young on their backs. And how they just make you say ooh and aww. With how adorable they are. and you just want to pick up and cuddle with the babies. Even though they are animals.

14
The Golden Number

People always say they have a lucky number. Breana's favorite number is 14 it is very special to her. Because that is the day she was born. The day where her crazy journey began on the earth. The day her parents got to meet her. Also that means when she turned 14 that was her golden birthday.

And when she ran track she wanted that to be her number on her jersey but she didn't get it. But that is okay. She always wanted to have her lucky number just like they do in the movies. But that is not very realistic. Just like in High School Musical. Troy Bolton has the number 16 as his lucky number.

But everyone has that special number that means something different and unique to them. It may be your birthday. A favorite athlete's number. To remember a special person's birthday, or when they passed away.

But she thinks everyone's number has a different meaning or story behind it. So what is your special number? Write it down somewhere and tell her what it means to you. It could mean a lot of things but is your special number. Just like all of us can't share the same fingerprints. Because we were all created differently and no one can ever be the same.

15
The Current Pets

Her pets right now she has a pet Betta fish . It is like a dark blue and purple fish. It lives all by itself in its small tank. Because if you put two in the same tank they will kill each other. Which is really crazy. Because most fish swim together in a school . Just like goldfish they do fine in the same tank. Inside her fish tank there are small red pebbles and it has a fake turtle. It is the character from Finding Nemo Crush the little turtle.

She also has a dog that is her whole families. He is a yorkie terrier. His name is ollie and he is only a puppy . He is very hyper and playful . He loves to chew on stuffed animals and rip them apart. He also loves to play and tries to bite . He likes to go on walks and gets scared when he sees larger dogs. And he won't go near them . Especially the neighbor dog who is big and is behind a fence. Also Ollie likes to try to beg for food. And likes to lay with you on the couch. He loves to get dog treats and chew on dog bones. She doesn't have any pets anymore the fish died and dogs went to other homes.

16
The Color

Her favorite color is blue like the bright sky. Or the big blue ocean that you see when you go to the beach. As the blue waves crash against the shore. Because this color just makes her feel all warm and happy inside.

When she sees it she just loves it in anything she sees it in. So like if she was in the car and she saw another car that was blue. She would focus on that car. Until it drove away And if she sees a blue jay or blue butterfly she is amazed by the bright color.

The brightness draws her in. The bright pigments she sees makes her light up. She loves that there are different shades of blue. There are light and dark shades of blue.

She loves to wear the color blue a lot . And she has a lot of blue things in her bedroom. Her bedspread is a teal blue she has teal blue signs that have inspirational sayings on them. She has one that says hope. And another one that says live, laugh ,love. And on the final sign says in our family we have faith. Believe in grace trust in God Expect Miracles and Give thanks Pray
always and Love One Another Choose Joy. Her Football team has the color blue on their jerseys . Her phone case is blue .

17
Under Pressure

Breana feels like she is always under pressure. Just like she always has something heavy hanging over her. Like a giant cylinder of cement.

Just because she is the oldest. And she feels that her parents and family expect so much from her. And she just wants to do the best she can. So that they are happy and not upset.

Like when you play a sport for example you feel pressure to win a certain game. By either you coach, parents or team. Well that is how she feels just by her family. She just wants to do something to make them proud. And she does not want to fail and let them down. She feels as if she fails at anything the pressure will push on her even more.
And they will be disappointed.

This is one of her fears and insecurities . Because she just wants to make them proud. To know that she accomplished successes and their approval .

18
The Bucket List

You know everyone has one of these. It is the list of dreams and aspirations. Where we list anything we want to accomplish in our lifetime. Some things are realistic while others will probably never happen.

Well for starters, all you need is a piece of paper and a pen. And you make a list of maybe ten things you would like to accomplish.
They can be simple of more complex it does not matter.

For Breana she has a list and she will tell you. Something may happen and she will feel accomplished and fulfilled. While other things may never come true.
So here is her list.

- Go to Egypt

Because she wants to see all the pyramids and Hieroglyphics. Because she is a huge nerd when it comes to history. Ever since she was a kid she fell in love with the subject. She used to want to be an archaeologist or anthropologist. But her plans changed.

- Go to New York to see the famous attraction the Statue of Liberty. Because it looks really cool and it is a part of history.

- Skydive indoors

Because if she really goes she could die instantly. Since her heart can not withstand the elevation in the air.

- Make several books and become a number 1 selling author

She enjoys and thrives to become an amazing writer.

- Go to Niagara Falls

Because she has seen it in movies and shows and it just looks beautiful .And to hear and see the large water falling.

- Go to a concert

To one of her favorite artists because she has never gone. Since they cost a lot of money .

- Go to the OSU Football game

It looks very exciting and she loves football , So it would be perfect for her. To finally be able to cheer of her favorite college team. And to be a fan yelling in the crowd . When they score touchdowns and when they get a pick six. And make a touchdown and beat the other team.

- Create a foundation

She wants to name it The Robin Ezekiel Legacy .
It would be a foundation for children who are fighting for a second chance at life. And to grant them a dream and turn it into a reality. Because nothing is impossible as long as you believe you can achieve. To name it after her teacher and little brother. Who she misses dearly.

- Go to a UFC fight

She loves watching them on tv . But to experience it in person would be awesome. Her all time favorite UFC fighter is Ronda Rousey . Because she set the bar for all Women who are now in the sport.

- Go to Corpus Christi . To see Selena's Museum and her fashion store. Ever since Breana has listened to her music and watched the movie she has always wanted to go visit .

So that is her list of everything she hopes to accomplish . Some of the things may never happen . But that is okay. As long as some of them get checked off . Then she can add more things and dreams .
She really hopes to make a foundation and become the number one selling author one day. I mean how hard can it be. To accomplish her dreams and desires. Everyone in the world has a bucket list that defines who they are. And who they want to become and everything they desire. She hopes everyone wants to make their own list. And try to do everything in their power to achieve them . All the dreams that are possible.

19
Family Game Night

When you hear about a game night. You imagine a bunch of people playing board games. Like Sorry , Apples to Apples , Monopoly. Or charades and Pictionary. Where you have to act out the games and guess the clues.

Breana and her family have a special board game . It is like the game Aggravation but it is a giant wooden board. Where you put your different colors of marbles on the board. And each player uses their marbles to try to get home by eating the other players marbles. But to do that each player has to roll a dice and get a one or a six to move out of the space. This game is a family tradition passed down to Breana's dad . From his Great Grandma Ofelia .

Her and her family also plays Mexican Bingo . Which is called Loteria . Each player has a card . And they use beans to cover up the images just like with regular bingo they use dotters. But each card has different images but they are in Spanish instead of English. She loves playing games with her family because they love to compete against each other.

20
Favorite Foods

Her favorite breakfast is French Toast . She found a really easy online recipe she follows to make it for her and her family. She loves to make it and cut up bananas and strawberries as the toppings . And the best part is to pour the nice and delicious syrup on top. And have a nice glass of white milk to wash all the sweetness down.

Her favorite meal is pizza . Because she loves the taste and all the vibrant colors. Just when you see a painting the abstract bright colors catch your eye. Especially when it is a painting of a food you want to eat the page.

And how her taste buds explode in her mouth. With all the different flavors . Just like in the movie *Ratatouille.* When the rat combines the fruit and cheeses together the flavors look like fireworks.
And she can decide what toppings and choices she wants to put on the pizza. Her favorite pizza is a Supre . Because it has pepperonis, and sausage , cheese and green bell peppers. And the crust is nice and doughy and soft as the cheese melts in your mouth.

And lastly the best part dessert. For dessert she enjoys eating ice cream. The richness of the cream goes perfectly together. Her favorite ice cream is probably cookie dough . Because it has tiny chunks of cookie dough and that combine well with the sweet vanilla flavored ice cream.

21
Friends

Breana has a few friends because she is not very social. But on her last year she met some amazing group of girls. They were a few grades below her . But that does not matter. They were the first friends where she felt like they were meant to be . Just like on the *Sisterhood of the Traveling Pants.* Where their friendship lasted with a pair of pants. But with Breanna and her friends they could tell each other anything. And they reminded her of all her old from Elementary and Middle School.

Her friends were awesome . She doesn't think her last year would of been so memorable without them. They would have sleepovers and watch movies and eat popcorn and junk food.
But now as she has graduated and works all the time she barely sees them. Except for M who she sees everyday at work.

Which is kind of cool to work at the same place as your best friend. Her other two friends are always at school . So she never gets to see them.

She just saw her friend Courtney and they finally caught up with each other. They spent a whole day with each other . They went to a Chinese Buffet . That had a bunch of options to choose from .

And you could have as much as you wanted. Then they had Velvet ice cream for dessert. Then they went to Toys R us to see everything that they had . Because it is fun looking at all their cool toys . Lastly, they went bowling it was really fun. Breana won most of the rounds. But they still had a great time . She can't wait till all of the friends can hang out all together just like old times.

She also has one other friend who she met because of her mom. When her mom worked at a bank her friend had a sister who was the same age and grade as Breana . They meet at an H's surprise birthday party and are best of friends ever since.

They went to the same school for a whole year. And they would do everything together go shopping hang out and watch tv shows especially *The Vampire Diaries* and *The Originals.* Because the lead actors are very good looking. And have sleepovers and go to H's sister's house to play volleyball and hide and seek.

Then they would go on car rides to get ice cream . Breana would watch H 's other sister kids. So that her sister could go to work and school .
But now she barely gets to see her. Because she has work and her friend is in college. But now H is a mom of a little girl named Thea .

Breana lives in Colorado now. So Breana sent her a baby gift since she couldn't be there when she was born.

Breana chose not to take that career path. She just felt like college was never for her. All her friends from colorado applied and had many scholarships from sports and academics. So they got into school .

But Breana never imagined going away to college to get a degree. She is more of the free spirited type. Who works and does the best she can at her job. And in her free time tries to accomplish her goals and dreams.

And she would rather not have to worry and stress about grades and passing semesters and terms. She did all of that enough in high school. Maybe one day she will change her mind . And try to go to school . But she would not know what should would want to major in. So for now she will just stay working .

22
The Beach

When you imagine the beach in your mind. You picture the nice hot sand going in between your toes. And the blue waves crashing against the shore. And all the different kinds of seashells that you pick that are washed up on the shore. She has collected a whole mason jar full of seashells. She has many kinds of shells . Her favorite ones are the spiral cone shaped ones. And took the sand from the beach in an empty water bottle.

Also , the huge sand castles that you can make with your family. And she bought a sweatshirt from a gift shop that says Myrtle Beach on it. And it is the color blue.

Breana has been to the beach a few times. Her favorite beach is Myrtle Beach. Because there are many attractions that you can go to. She went to the Medieval Times show before. It is really cool where people dress up like the Era . And they fight with jostes and rides horses. And do a lot of other tricks. And you and your family get to eat this large meal while you watch and enjoy the show. There's also a mini putt putt golf courses there are really fun.

She also has been to Daytona Beach which she also loves. Because the water is a lot clearer. And not very many people are on the beach. So it is not so crowded.

23
Fear is a Funny Thing

When you ride a roller coaster you fear the huge drop coming as you sit on the top. You hear the cranking sound on the coaster you know the drop is coming. Then as you drop the fear starts to go away as the adrenalin starts to kick in.

But when we fear something our emotions come out. It is like we can not control it . Your body starts to fear the unknown approaching. Your hairs on your body start to rise as your heart races.

And if you have ever seen *Fear Factor.* Where the contestants are tested on fear. To try to accomplish three obstacles to win the cash prize. But most of the contests go home on the first round because the fear of touching the animal or eating it scares them too much.

Or trying to get the flags from a driving car or a jet ski. And the one where they are locked in a cage underwater and the partner has to rescue them before they can come up for air.

But a lot of the contestants let their fear of drowning get in the way and they have to quit early before they can be rescued.

There are many things people fear and are very different from each other. Breana has a few fears. She does not like clowns because they are creepy .

And she does not like spiders or snakes . Because spiders have long legs and are fast. And snakes are giant and can swallow people whole. And she does not like mice . Because they are gross and hairy rodents.

And she will not go to a haunted house because she hears many stories about bad things happening. And she does not want scary people to chase her around with weapons. Especially when she doesn't want any clowns to pop out and get her.

Also she won't watch scary movies. Even though she knows they are just acting . Like all her friends and family love scary movies. And always want to see the new ones. But Breana would rather watch a comedy or animation film.

But fear can also be a good thing. Because if you fear about a certain outcome on a test or job. You might be afraid and think you will fail but then you actually pass the test . And get the job that you wanted.

So try something that you fear the most . And conquer it because only you can get over it. Like Breana, feared interviewing for the job she had . She did not think she could do the interview but she faced it and it went well and she has the job.
Some fear can be a bad thing or a temptation. Like when the devil tries to tempt you to disobeying your parents.

Or how when a friend tries to peer pressure you into going to a party that has drinking. You fear that if you don't go to the party you will lose a friend.
But that is not true it is just the devil playing tricks in your head. To want you to rebel and sin.

"Just like in the bible when the devil tried to make Jesus afraid and to make him sin." "But he stood his ground and used the word of God against him so Satan would go away."

It is really cool that her pastor did a message all on fear. And she wrote a chapter about it the night before. That is kind of ironic to write all about fear and then he preached about the same topic. And the chapter had a lot of similar concepts and ideas.

24
Imagination

You know how people say it is just their imagination. So like little kids use their imagination a lot. To make up make believe characters. And imaginary friends .

Breana likes to do that when she is writing her stories. Her characters can travel to make believe worlds . And then her imagination comes to life off the page. Just as if the characters were real people. And if they could really jump out of the page just like as a cartoon .
But as a kid your imagination can be anything you can dream of. Like if you have ever seen *The Adventures of Sharkboy and Lavagirl* . It is a movie based on dreams and endless imagination. And where his dreams actually come to life . And help to save the planet.

Also your imagination goes along with your dreams and goals in life. Because as a kid you imagine being an astronaut or cop. And that is the career and person you aspire to be. But as you grow up that imagination slowly fades and the real goal or career you want changes.
And instead of imagining things you start having visions and dreams. Just like in Joel 2:28 "And it shall come to pass afterward, I will pour out my spirit upon all flesh; and your sons and daughters shall prophesy, your old men shall dream dreams, your young men shall see visions."
And the dream you wanted starts to go away . For Breana she always aspired to be a writer . And she was going to make it possible no matter what challenges were thrown in her direction. No matter if people told her that was silly and her writing will never be good enough.
She just kept imagining that one day her dream could be possible. And that was all she needed to keep her dream and hope alive.

25
Temptations

When a person is tempted they usually turn away from God and sin. Just like in Adam and Eve. When they were tempted by the forbidden fruit but it looked delicious and the serpent told them to try it. So out of temptation they sinned and were banished from the Garden of Eden.

So as people we are tempted easily by the things that we see everyday. Like when we see something on tv we have an urge to buy it.

And especially by peer pressure when your friends try and make you do bad things. Thankful Breana was raised right and to not listen when others try to get her to sin and party. Instead she never went to a school party because she knew drinking can lead to bad things. It is bad for your body and it can harm a lot of people if you are not of age and have it responsibility.

In Matthew 6 :13 says " And lead us not into temptation, but deliver us from evil , For thine is the kingdom, and the power , and the glory , forever. Amen."

26
Anger and Hurt

Ecclesiastes 7:9 (KJV) says "Be not hasty in thy spirit to be angry: for anger resteth in the bosom of fools."

In Proverbs 15:1 says "A soft answer turneth away wrath: but grievous words stir up anger".

She has been hurt many times in her past . She feels that is why she closes herself off from friends and family. Because she has lost her ability to trust. Because of that she finds it hard to open up to people.

If she does she fears they will hurt her. Just like so many people that she loves have done before. And because of that she closes herself off and becomes really depressed . But no one notices because she keeps her emotions and insecurities bottled away.

And because of that she has thought of suicidal thoughts but nobody knew. Because she felt so low and worthless that she just wanted all the pain to end and go away. But she knew that is a sin and she rather live another day. Just like the song that is by Logic to prevent those thoughts is called 1- 800.
Also she listens to Lecrae Can't' stop me now . It is a song about being depressed. And doubting God and taking the depression away.

She has a lot of scars but they make her stronger. You can not visibly see all the scars , because they are covered in bandages. And are inside of her body . Just like when you get a papercut it is so small you can barely see it.
The scars you can see are from her surgery and are clearly visible.
And when that happens she kind of shuts down and hides from the world.
Because she would rather keep all her hurt and pain locked away.

And then she writes all her feelings and emotions down . Since she has no one she trusts or to vent too. All the people she thought were there for her abandoned her . And they turned on her when she needed them the most.

27
Forgiveness and Healing

She has realized that being angry can not be healthy. So she has decided that she has to move on from the past . And push through all the pain. Even though some situations were really tough . She has to find it in her heart to forgive. That is the only way she can find healing.

Just as the scripture Ephesians 4:32 says in “And be ye kind one to another, tenderhearted, forgiving one another, even as God for Christ's sake hath forgiven you.”

And listened to Kesha’s new song *Praying* . She loves to listen to the lyrics and it helps her bring closure and healing . Because it is all about facing the monsters in the world. And that God can only judge and can forgive for all the bad a person has done.

The final song she listens to is *Forgive me* by Group One Crew. It is about asking God for forgiveness when you have sinned .

And that God is always there when we need him .“He will never leave or forsake us.”(Deuteronomy 31:6.)

“'He healeth the broken in heart, and bindeth up their wounds.' When we are hurt and broken God takes all the pain away.”
(Psalms 147. 3)

Just like the song *Broken Vessels* by Hillsong United. It talks about being broken and how God is a vessel for our life. And how he can take all are failures and weaknesses away.

28
Struggles and Triumph

Everyone struggles with something in their life. But for Breana everything she has struggled with she turned it into a victory instead of defeat. She struggled in school but that did not stop her from getting good grades and graduating. And when she ran track everyone thought that was crazy. because she was not athletic . But she proved them all wrong and earned A Varsity Letter.

Many people struggle with something different . Like depression, loneliness, anger , fear.

She has struggled with most of these things especially depression. For her she just gets so down and feels worthless . And she lets all of her emotions get the best of her at times. To her it is a deep insecurity she tries to hide. Instead of letting people know.
By smiling all the time and when people ask she just puts on a smile . So they won't ask how she is . Because to them she seems fine.

And if someone does ask she denies it . Because she does not want to let them feel bad for her . And she does not trust very many people because so many have ruined that feeling for her.

And she struggles with anger as said earlier.
Many of are struggles come from are past . And so we carry them with us. Instead of letting them go and conquering them.

She has learned to accept all of her struggles and do the best to live life and be victorious. And to live triumphantly like you are winning at life. And in all her struggles and defeats she knows God will always provide and has her back no matter what .

In 1 Thessalonians 5:16 -18 it says “Be Joyful always, pray continually,give thanks in all circumstances, for this is God’s will for you in Christ Jesus.”

Just like the song *It's the climb* by Miley Cyrus from the Hannah Montana Movie. Talks all about struggles and having faith but to just keep pushing past the mountain.

Also she listens to *I look to you* by the legendary artist Whitney Houston. Because it is about struggles and how we can not overcome them without the help of God. He is the only one who has the power to help heal our wounds and make us whole again. And to lead us back to his path.

29
Regrets

Many people say to life life to the fullest with no regrets. But as a human being you will have many regrets in life and mistakes. Because we are not meant to be perfect. We are meant to make mistakes and that is okay.

For her she has a lot of regrets she wishes she could change. But the thing is you can't change is the past. You can only change what is to come in the future. And all the baggage from the past that you carry through life molds you into the person you are today.

Because without all the struggles you face their would be no regrets in life. She wishes some things she could change like all the bad decisions she made will just disappear.

But all are regrets are permanent just like a tattoo or birthmark and a sharpie marker.

That is why people say don't get a tattoo that you will regret. Because you are permanently marked and it won't come off with soap and water. Instead you will have to live with that choice forever.
That is why Breana's tattoos are both something meaningful to her life. And with a sharpie marker you can not erase it . So the thing you draw or write is stuck on the paper forever. Same as a birthmark it is on your body forever because it is how you are made .

And some things she regrets in life is if she went to college. Instead of just working all the time.
But all the regrets and mistakes have and impact and a powerful meaning

in her life.

Because we are not perfect we are suppose to mess up and make mistakes. God is the only one who was perfect. And to him we are perfect in his image. So just remember all you regrets and mistakes you have the power to control them .

And you are the one who has to live with the guilt and the what if's . So don't live your life in fear of regrets and mistakes. Life it to the fullest because we only live once.

30
Memories

Have you heard the saying memories last a lifetime. Well that saying is mostly true. Breana has a lot of memories. Some are good while others she wishes she could forget.

She loves all her memories of spending time with Mrs. G .With all the laughs and cries they had. She will cherish all those wonderful memories forever.

And all her memories of spending time with her family going swimming and on family vacations. And taking silly pictures together.

And all the memories of her and her friends got to create. WIth their laughs and cries while talking . Also their time they got to spend with each other even though it was only for a year . But she has some bad memories she wishes she could forget. Like when others bullied her in school because she was shy. Especially teachers they can be so cruel . Even though they are suppose to help kids grow with their education. Being bullied is the worst feeling in the world. She wishes she could of just stood up for herself when was picked on . But ever since then she vowed to not let people put her down and now she is stronger than ever. Not to let their words and actions affect her anymore.

The End

God works in mysterious ways

It's crazy how God works in mysterious ways . Tonight I recieved a little bible from one of my customers who I didn't even know. But it's like God knew I needed to read the bible more. And he sent this customer. I mean, lately I have not been wanting to go to church or read the Bible . Because I have been dealing with depression and anger and anxiety. That I try to hide and keep to myself. And it's like the movie Inside Out where all the emotions are yelling at each other that is like me right now. Then that I really don't have any friends to hang out with and always alone I get really depressed. That the fact when you start to turn away from God and feel at your lowest moment in life. He finds a way to lift you up and out of the darkness . So I was struggling and he sent this customer to be my guardian angel . Who he sent to me because God will always lead you back to him.

Normally I would not open myself up cause Im a personal person especially with my feelings . But I thought their are other people who I could help . And others that can relate or had a similar experience in their life.

Poem of life

Her life has been a crazy ride .
just as a skateboarder riding through the street.
flying high in the heat
listening to a sick beat
doing ollies and kickflips
off a ramp
she just wants to make a stamp
and make a mark
just like a skid mark
at the skatepark
make her mark known
and inspire others
to make their own mark
by Alexis Gutierrez

Doctors Visit

A year ago she recently had to be rushed to the ER. They are saying something could be wrong with her heart again. Because she passed out at work and threw up. And she was as pale as a ghost. So they gave her an IV in the left arm and she returned back to normal color. And they did an EKG test and said that the numbers are off . From the last time she had it done. So now she has to sit at home and wait till she can see her cardiologist to make sure everything is okay. And they also took two samples of blood work. So for now she is off of work until they can see what is wrong. But she thinks it is stress related. Since she is ironically starting College in a few days and it is nerve racking but I know I will be alright. And she has to pay for a lot of things . And at work has to watch ten toddlers all by herself and never get a break or day off.

New Poem

I've been so depressed and such a mess

laying in bed rest

cause they are saying something is wrong with my chest

please God I'm begging you on my knees heal my body please

the devil is attacking me and making me drown

But I know God will reach his hand down and save me again

and take all this pain away

cause I'm here to stay

I have to go get more blood drawn today hopefully everything will come out okay. And that they will give me a note so I can return back to work . So that I can earn some money so I can start paying for college. Because I have to pay back a student loan . Since I started my first day of college in a few days. And if they do a test for my chest that everything will come back to normal. Because being home is starting to drive me crazy. I am ready to begin college and try something new.

And finally maybe meet some friends that are my age. And to get out of the house and do normal activities again instead of just resting and staying home all day long. So God please let everything come back normal and fine . And that I can make the payment on time. In Jesus name Amen. Finally saw a cardiologist today and I didn't have to do any tests. No EKG and No ECO cardiogram. And he said everything looked good .

And he said it was mainly stressed related why I passed out and got sick and had to go to the ER for six hours.

So he said it is my best interests to stop working at my job and to focus on school. And to find another job that will ease the stress. So hopefully when I leave this job and talk with the Boss it will go smoothly. And hopefully I will get one of the positions at the college. So I am praying for favor and courage. In Jesus name amen.

First week of college in the books

First week of college was a success ! At the NJC in Sterling , Co. In my first class we made playdough with lotion . And we drew with chalk and vinegar outside . Also we got to eat Cheerios and fruit snacks and made a picture out of them that would make us happy. So I made flowers.

And every other class we had to talk notes and do in class discussions. Also I went to Starbucks and got a small Vanilla Bean to make my week even better.

And I am also taking an independent study class to do at my own pace.

So all my nerves for school have all went away . And I also got a free shirt for the college.

Now I am just waiting to see if my teacher will put my grades in. And all my health is doing good for now just trying not to stress out too much. With working in the morning to going to college in the afternoon.

Now just waiting to get new glasses because I am way overdue for a new pair and a check up.

First Month of College

So far school has been okay. And when people say college is easy they are lying because I am so stressed out right now I am reaching my max . I am trying so hard to succeed so I can get my certificate . But my advice is that if you are going to go in school then you should go right after High School And not to wait till you are in your 20 's .

Midterms

My Midterms are coming up this week feeling very anxious and worried.

I hate taking tests.

But I think as long as I study and not think of it as a huge test I will be okay.

Just have to keep my head up and pray that God gives me the knowledge and wisdom to pass them!

College Finals Week Semester 1 Yikes !

This week is my first week of finals ! I am freaking out because they are so much of my grade! And it's my first year and first semester of college..... So I am just praying that God will give me the strength and wisdom and knowledge that I need to pass all of my classes. I just took my first one today and winged it so hopefully I passed it and two more to go on Thursday back to back ! I have so much stress and anxiety and work has been bad lately I might end up with a panic attack!!!!!!!!!! And then I get to be done and go on vacation and come back and do more school !! With work it been so crazy I don't know how much longer I can hang on ! Please God just pray I can pass before I run into the glass ! Well I passed one class so far with a 90 percent! I am still waiting till the last two finals are graded! I hate the waiting game but I probably won't know until Monday night the 17th !! So know I just have to be patient and pray that everything is in God's hands !

And as long as I pass each class and pass my very first semester of college that all that counts ! And looked at my GPA as of right now have a 4.00 hopeful I can pass the other finals to keep it that way !

This semester has gone by so fast I can't believe in a few more months I will receive my college certificate for a Director for Early Childhood Education ! Actually that got delayed and had to add more classes and go another semester and getting 2 certifications.

So far have all A's in every class !

And Finished my Freshman seminar with a 100 %.

I also got a 4.0 for my first semester and was on the President's List Honor Roll !!

When your stressed out !

When your stressed out and your trying to do your best

but you just need some rest

so that you can bless others

Feeling so stressed out again just started a new semester of college 2019

and it's not one thing it's another its homework or work

my body is starting to go numb

where its starting to tingle before you start to pass out or have a panic attack

people keep asking me to help them with school which is OK

and I am having trouble with my classes this semester they are a lot trickier than I thought.

But I know I am I can do all things through Christ who strengthens me Philippians 4 :13

And just take my time and go at my own pace, I know I can complete and run this crazy race to the finish line again and get another 4.0 .

Blessed

Today is Christmas the most wonderful time of the year ! Where you celebrate the life of Jesus and spend the day with your family ! And you do get presents but that's not what Christmas is about . I am truly grateful and blessed because my middle sister flew down last night from Ohio to visit. And I get to spend the whole week with her then we fly home to Ohio and I get to see my friends and parents and my baby sister !!! So I would say this year I am very grateful to be here with my family and friends and my Big Grandpa !

And I just spoke to my mom and I told her how when I come back on vacation my family and I are working on buying my brother his tombstone. Finally, since it's been 18 years that's he's been gone .But I know he is watching from above. Mom said as she got teary eyed and told me that my middle sister Allyah randomly brought it up that he needs a stone since it's been so long . I can't wait to buy him one when I return from vacation. To go buy him one and pick it out. The crazy thing is this year would of been his senior year ! And when I turned 18 I got my first tattoo to remember him !!!

Grief and the Five Stages

Going through grief is the hardest thing anyone has to experience. Take it from me personally I have lost enough loved ones it is hard to bear. I just lost my pastor who meant so much to me and his family is like my second family.

Pastor was a Great Pastor who we will all miss dearly
He was taken to soon
I have many great memories from the time I was born and prayed for after having open heart surgery
to staying the night with his family and growing up playing with the kids
He was a very genuine soul
who had a big heart
and loved teaching God's word
And always smiling and giving high fives
Ik he is smiling up above
As he is entering the kingdom of God
His memories and legacy will live on through
his children and grandchildren
So sorry for the family and their loss
with all love Lexi ❤

Grief goes in 5 stages

The First stage is shock you don't know what hit you just freeze. And you just can't move or express the loved one is truly gone. And death comes so unexpected just as life comes into the world it can also be taken.

Second stage is emotion and your whole body can't express that the loved one is gone ! And you just mourn for days or years .

Third stage is anger because sometimes you don't get to tell the loved one goodbye and never will get the chance to until the day you can be reunited.

The Fourth stage is Unexplained happiness you begin to laugh over all the good times you had with the person. And cry of laughter instead of sadness.

The Fifth stage is accepting that the loved one is gone ! Each person grieves in their own way. But accepting that they are gone and not suffering anymore or they are gone and happy is the hardest thing to do.

Here to the New Year 2019

Everyone says to make reflections and goals but I am just going to go this year as a New me and taken. Also to just take it one day at a time and be blessed every day of life I get to live !
And to cherish all the good times and laughs and cries of the New Year.
And all the friends that I have and that I get to see this year !
And all the joy and happiness God will bless me with this year !
This year I am officially taken and have a man in my life for the first time ! I can finally say I'm not single anymore ! We meet at school !

Not My Lucky Day

Do you ever have just a bad day .Well that was me yesterday I was at college walking home from the campus and slipped and fell on a piece of ice . As I was going down hoping no one saw me wishing I caught it on snapchat .And it was like that awkward kind of fall. Not like on your bottom like where you do the weird kind of splits. And I fell on my bad knee that still bothers me from track . So now it's all bruised and I am feeling the pain and affects from it today .The only good thing is that when I get hurt I just laugh things off instead of cry. So after I fell I got up busted out laughing and walked home. Then when I came back to school for the next class I told them I fell. Then when that class ended I was waiting for my aunt to pick me up when another student slipped on the ice but she caught herself before she slipped and almost ran into the trash can.

Calm Before the Storm

I've gotta keep the calm before the storm
I don't want less, I don't want more
Must bar the windows and the doors
To keep me safe, to keep me warm
Yeah my life is what I'm fighting for
Can't part the sea, can't reach the shore
And my voice becomes the driving force
I won't let this pull me overboard
God, keep my head above water
Don't let me drown, it gets harder
I'll meet you there at the altar
As I fall down to my knees
Don't let me drown, drown, drown
Don't let me, don't let me, don't let me drown
So pull me up from down below
'Cause I'm underneath the undertow
Come dry me off and hold me close
I need you now I need you most
God, keep my head above water
Don't let me drown, it gets harder
I'll meet you there at the altar
As I fall down to my knees
Don't let me drown, drown, drown
(Don't let me, don't let me, don't let me drown)
Don't let me drown, drown, drown
And keep my head above water
(Don't let me, don't let me, don't let me drown) by Avril Lavigne

So everyone always knows the saying calm before the storm . These past few weeks was calm then it went into a giant storm . My Uncle Joe who I didn't get to see all the time . I went to see him and he was sick and before I knew it we had his funeral which was unexpected.

But I know he is at peace in rest in God's kingdom. Because the night he passed it rained so hard its like you knew he went home with God. But I am forever grateful to get to talk with him about football and his collection and mine.

And at that moment I started to cry and especially when they played the song Remember Me from Coco . And I just kind of lost and I never cried at any funerals that I have been to I usually cry before or after its over . Matthew 5.4 kJV(Blessed are they that mourn, for they shall be comforted.)

Then after that because I was gone I was behind on school and my grades dropped to a B. And I was trying to catch up and bring them back up to A and thankfully did it at the end and the stormed passed. But now my heart murmur came back again so hoping it will go away again on its own .

Acknowledgments

Mom, you are awesome thank you for giving me life. And for your love and encouragement through all my journeys and for always being there when I need someone to lean on. For, being my life coach and my best friend. And my person always .

Dad, thanks for always pushing me to try and not give up. For always watching wrestling with me. For your delicious and amazing food. And all your great wisdom.

Allyah, you are a great sister someone I love hanging out with. And going shopping with because you know what fashion trends .

Ady, you are a great little sister and I happy love your great personality that you have.

Notes

Introduction

1.“David and Goliath - 1 Samuel 17 - KJV.” EBible, ebible.com/kjv/section/472.

2.“Book of Esther – Read the Bible Online.” Bible Study Tools, www.biblestudytools.com/esther/.

3. Jeremiah 29:11

https://www.bible.com/bible/1/JER.29.11

Ch. 4 Real Life begins

1. “Philippians 4:13 - KJV - I Can Do All Things through Christ Which Strength...” Bible Study Tools, www.biblestudytools.com/kjv/philippians/4-13.html.

2. “Hope has come” by Once Church Music .published. Dec.25 , 2015.

Ch. 6 Hobbies and Collections

1. TEBOW, TIM. SHAKEN: Discovering Your True Identity in the Midst of Life's Storms. WATERBROOK PR, 2017.

TV Shows.

1. “Grey's Anatomy” , 2. “Chicago Med”, 3. “PD”. 4. “Fire”. 5. “Total Bellas”, 6. “Total Divas”

Artists 1.Lecree

2. Tori Kelly 3.Mariah Carey. 4.Selena Quintanilla.

1. Songs “Bye Bye” by Mariah Carey published. Jun 16, 2009.
2. “I will find you” by Lecrae , Featuring , Tori Kelly. published. Jul 28 , 2017.

3. Director .Ayer , David. Suicide Squad . August 1, 2016. DC Entertainment. Distributed by Warner Bros Pictures.

Ch.8 The Reflection in the mirror

1. Bancroft, Tony, Cook, Barry director. *Mulan.* Walt Disney Pictures, Walt Disney Feature Animation. , 1998.
2. "Man in the mirror "by Michael Jackson published. 2009.
3. Romans 8:28

https.www.bible.com/bible/1/ROM/8.28

Ch. 10 the Holiday

1. Favreau, Jon, director. "Elf." New Line Cinema, 2003.
2. Roth, Joe, director. "Christmas with the Kranks." Columbia Pictures, 2004.
3. Hughes, John. "*Home Alone.*" Twentieth Century Fox, 1990.
4. Gordon, Seth, director. Four Christmases. Spyglass Entertainment, 2008.
5. Pasquin, John, director. Santa Clause .Disney. 1994.

Ch.12 Celebrations

1. Director, Burton, Tim. Charlie and the Chocolate Factory

Ch. 13 Favorite Animal

2. Wyatt, Rupert, director. *Rise of the Planet of the Apes* . 20th Century Fox. 2011.

Ch.14 the Golden Number

1. Ortega, Kenny, director. *High School Musical.* Disney. 2006.

Ch. 20 Favorite Food

1. Bird, Brad Pinkava , Jan , director. Ratatouille .Disney. 2007.

Ch. 21 Friends

1. Plec, Julie , Executive Producer. *The Vampire Diaries* . The CW Network. 2013-present.

2. Williamson, Kevin, Plec, Julie, Executive Producer .*The Originals.* The CW Network. 2009-present.

3. Kwapis , Ken director. *The Sisterhood of the Traveling Pants.* Warner Bros. Pictures . June 3 ,2005.

Ch.23 Fear is a funny thing

1. Morgan, Joe, Host. Fear Factor . Reality Game show. NBC. 2001-2012.

Ch.24 Imagination

1. Rodriguez , Robert director. *The Adventures of Sharkboy and Lavagirl* . Columbia Pictures Corporation. June 10,2005.
2. Joel 2:28
   https://www.bible.com/bible/1/JOE/2.28

Ch.25 Temptations

1. Matthew 6:13

https://ww.bible.com/bible/MAT/6:13

Ch.26 Anger and Hurt

1. "1 -800 -273-8255" by Logic feat. Alessia Cara , Dj. Kahlid . Published Aug 27,2017.
2. "Can't Stop me now"(Destination) by Lecrae . Published .Oct 21,2016.
3. "Praying" by Kesha . (Rainbow Album) . Published Jul 6 , 2017 .
4. Ecclesiastes 7:9
   https://www.bible.com/bible/1/ECC.7:9

5. Ephesians 4:31
https://www.bible.com/bible/1/EPH.4.31
6. Matthew 6:13
https://ww.bible.com/bible/1/MAT/6.13

Ch.27 Forgiveness and Healing

1. "Forgive me" by Group One Crew . Published on Jun 14 , 2007.
2. Deuteronomy 31 :6
https://www.bible.com/bible/1/DEU.31.6
3. Ephesians 4:32
https://www.bible.com/bible/1/EPH.4.31
4. Psalms 147:3
https://www.bible.com/bible/1/PSA.147.3
5. Broken Vessels By Hillsong United. Published . June, 1 2017.

Ch.28 Struggles and Triumph

1. 1 Thessalonians 5:16 -18
https://www.bible.com/bible/1/THE.5.16-18.

2. "It's the climb" by Miley Cyrus from the Hannah Montana Movie produced by Chelesom, Peter . April 10,2009.

3. I Look to you by Whitney Houston. Published November 14, 2009.

Ch. 30 Memories

1. 1 Timothy 6:9
https://www.bible.com/bible/1/TIM/6.9.
2. 1 Timothy 6:10
https:www.bible.com/bible/1/TIM/6.10

Calm Before the Storm

1.Head Above Waters by Avril Lavigne published September 27 , 2018.
2.Matthew 5.4 kjv
https://www.kingjamesbibleonline.org/Matthew-5-4/
3. Director , Lee Unkrich, Adrian Molina Movie Coco Released November 22 , 2017 .

Author Note

Thank you to all my readers for choosing this book to read . Hope you enjoyed it and hopefully more books to come in the future . And thank you to everyone who has read it on Wattpad and for giving me all the reads and making my dream possible.

This book is signed by the author

Alexis Gutierrez

www.ingramcontent.com/pod-product-compliance
Ingram Content Group UK Ltd.
Pitfield, Milton Keynes, MK11 3LW, UK
UKHW020138250726
13967UKWH00002B/729

9 781716 965593